Pamela Harriman

A Life of Power, Passion, and Political Prowess

Eleanor T. Whitfield

Table of Contents

Introduction

Chapter 1: The Making of a Churchill

Chapter 2: A Wartime Marriage

Chapter 3: The Seductive Diplomat

Chapter 4: Seduction for Victory

Chapter 5: The Fiat Heir

Chapter 6: A Continental Affair

Chapter 7: The Move to America

Chapter 8: Rebuilding the Democratic Party

Chapter 9: Spotlighting Bill Clinton

Chapter 10: The Appointment to Ambassador

Chapter 11: Charm and Diplomacy in Paris

Chapter 12: Bosnia and the Peak of American Power

Chapter 13: Friends, Foes, and Lovers

Chapter 14: The Final Chapter: Power till the End

Introduction

The name Pamela Harriman may conjure up ideas of extravagant parties, high-profile weddings, and rumors of scandal; but, beyond the gloss, there was a lady who exercised great influence in the background. Even though she was sometimes seen as little more than a simple socialite or seductress, Harriman was a geopolitical thinker who altered the path that history took on both sides of the Atlantic.

To say that Pamela Harriman's life was a demonstration of the art of subtle persuasion would be an understatement. From her early days as Winston Churchill's daughter-in-law, discreetly influencing American opinion during

World War II, to her involvement in raising Bill Clinton to the president, Pamela Harriman's life was a tribute to the art.

It was not just her beauty that made her stand out in a society that was controlled by males; it was also her strong grasp of people, politics, and power that made her stand out. He was a power that was often unseen but always successful, whether he was eating with diplomats or negotiating behind closed doors. Harriman was effective in both situations.

She went from being the epitome of English to being one of the most powerful political powerbrokers in the United States, making an effect on international diplomacy that very few people have ever properly acknowledged.

Presented in this book is the genuine tale of Pamela Harriman, a lady whose legacy extends beyond the scandalous headlines and the misguided impressions that have been around her. In this story, charm was turned into a weapon, and relationships were used as instruments to influence the world. Additionally, it is a story about passion, strategy, and perseverance.

Chapter 1: The Making of a Churchill

He was the daughter of Edward Digby, the 11th Baron Digby, and Constance Pamela Alice Bruce, Pamela Beryl Digby was born on March 20, 1920, into the English nobility. Pamela Beryl Digby was the daughter of Edward Digby. Raised in the tradition of the British upper class, Pamela's upbringing was one of luxury, where riches and title granted a social rank that offered possibilities few could envision.

Yet, despite her privileged origins, the society into which Pamela was born was far from static—it was a moment of immense political and social upheaval. As the British Empire started its gradual collapse following the First

World War, a new breed of aristocrats was developing, one who had to manage the changing sands of global politics, public image, and power.

The Digby family's fortune was small by aristocratic standards, but its legacy was vast. The Digbys were among the landed gentry, maintaining authority over their family estates in Dorset, where Pamela grew up. The family preserved their position by careful management of these properties and the respect that comes with a noble heritage.

As a kid, Pamela was prepared for a life among the wealthy. She was schooled in the traditions of the upper class, attending private schools, and being exposed to the fine arts, etiquette, and the expectations of ladies of her station. However, it wasn't long before Pamela's beauty and irresistible charisma would outshine her inherited titles.

Her upbringing was typical of English aristocratic households at the period, with a deliberate balance of harsh discipline and the development of social elegance. Pamela's youth was spent on the family estate at Minterne Magna, surrounded by enormous grounds and old walls that appeared to encapsulate the weight of the Digby family's past.

But, although her family life was steeped with the trappings of the English aristocracy, her education, and socialization pointed to a far bigger world outside the limits of Dorset. Pamela's early years were spent under the shadow of her father's expectations, as he strove to turn her into the perfect lady of the upper class—an obedient bride, a helpful companion, and a social asset. But there was something about Pamela's personality that made her distinct from her contemporaries. She had an incredible capacity to interact with people, easily enchanting those around her with both her humor and attractiveness.

This expertise, paired with her dazzling beauty, would prove to be one of her greatest advantages in the decades to come, enabling her to form connections with some of the most prominent men of her day.

The Digby family's contacts with the nobility and the political elite meant that Pamela was exposed to high society from an early age. Her parents routinely hosted significant persons from

British political and social circles, and Pamela learned early on the importance of discussion and social involvement. This early exposure would eventually help her negotiate the intricate world of diplomacy and politics, where a well-timed phrase or a subtle gesture may have huge implications.

Her father, Baron Digby, was a quiet but dominant presence in her upbringing, instilling in her a feeling of obligation to family and nation. While he had a quiet disposition, he had lofty goals for Pamela, wanting her to marry well and perpetuate the family's history.

Meanwhile, her mother, Constance, epitomized the elegance and poise of the nobility, giving Pamela the sophisticated manners and social grace that would later serve her well in diplomatic circles. Constance's impact was especially significant in developing Pamela's knowledge of how to keep control and poise, even in the most trying social settings.

The Digbys were intimately linked to Winston Churchill, a friendship that would subsequently play a vital part in molding Pamela's life. The family link to Churchill provided Pamela a unique insight into the workings of British high society and the inner sanctum of political power.

It was via this relationship that she would meet Randolph Churchill, Winston's only son, a man who would change the course of her life and vault her from aristocratic luxury to the heart of one of Britain's most important families.

But Pamela's success wasn't only due to her family's connections. Even at an early age, she exhibited an inherent awareness of how to manage the complexity of human interactions, especially when it came to males.

Pamela was acutely aware of her beauty and charm, and she utilized both to her advantage. From an early age, she realized the significance of building strong friendships and putting herself in circles where influence could be wielded.

Early Life in England

Pamela's early existence in England was entrenched in the traditions of the nobility, but it was also affected by the fast-changing world around her. The 1920s and 1930s witnessed a major upheaval in the structure of British society, as the aftermath of World War I and the

Great Depression led to a reassessment of previous class systems. For the British aristocracy, this was a moment of both introspection and adaptation, and Pamela's upbringing represented this transitional age. She was reared in an atmosphere where the grandeur of the past was venerated, but the problems of modernity could not be disregarded.

Life on the family estate in Dorset was both magnificent and isolated. Minterne Magna was a remote estate, packed with the type of grandeur and isolation that offered Pamela the chance to immerse herself in the world of the elite.

Her family kept traditions that had been handed down for generations—fox hunting, extravagant dinner parties, and the social graces that were required of the English upper class. Yet, despite the beauty and affluence of this environment, there remained an underlying feeling of obligation that Pamela could not avoid. She was supposed to marry well, build connections, and maintain the family lineage.

Education for young ladies of Pamela's level was aimed not so much at intellectual growth as at preparing them to join society. Pamela attended many finishing schools, where she was taught how to communicate, entertain, and maintain the social duties of her class. These institutions were less about academics and more about shaping young women into the ideal wives and hostesses—roles that were important to the life of an aristocratic lady in pre-war England.

However, Pamela's schooling was not wholly traditional. She was an ardent reader, and her curiosity stretched well beyond the bounds of what was customarily taught to ladies of her class. She was captivated by politics, international affairs, and culture, things she would later utilize to her advantage in talks with some of the most influential men of her day.

Her capacity to participate in meaningful debate set her apart from other women of her background, establishing her as someone who might be more than simply a passive socialite.

As a young lady, Pamela was greatly inspired by the political scene of the period. The interwar years were a time of major change in Britain, with the advent of fascism in Europe and the continued impacts of the Great Depression. These worldwide events had a dramatic effect on the aristocracy, as many families, like the

Digbys, saw their money and power eroding. But while other families withdrew their money and prestige, Pamela recognized a chance to adapt and succeed in a changing world.

In 1938, at the age of 18, Pamela made her formal entrance into London society, signifying her admission into the realm of aristocratic balls, parties, and high society gatherings. She rapidly became a fixture of the London social scene, charming everyone around her with her beauty and charm. Her initial season was a triumph, and Pamela's name was immediately associated with numerous significant personalities, but none more important than Randolph Churchill, Winston Churchill's son.

Randolph was a fascinating and disturbed character, noted for his strong attitude and unpredictable conduct. Despite his weaknesses, he was the heir of one of Britain's most respected political families, and his relationship with Winston Churchill made him an alluring proposition for any young lady. It wasn't long before Pamela and Randolph got intimately entangled, a connection that would eventually bring her into the heart of British politics.

In 1939, as Europe teetered on the verge of war, Pamela married Randolph Churchill. This marriage was not merely a union of two individuals but the blending of two great families.

With this marriage, Pamela's life would alter forever. She would transition from being Pamela Digby, a member of the nobility, to Pamela

Churchill, a lady whose destiny rested at the heart of British and world power.

Chapter 2: A Wartime Marriage

Pamela Digby was born into British nobility on March 20, 1920, in Farnborough, Hampshire. She was nurtured in a milieu of affluence, but one formed by the strict social systems of her day. Her father, Edward Digby, the 11th Baron Digby, and her mother, Constance, instilled in her the significance of rank, etiquette, and navigating the labyrinthine webs of British society.

While her childhood was wealthy, it did not foresee the enormous destiny that awaited her. It was World War II that changed her from a farm child into a pivotal figure in both British and American history.

Pamela's moment to ascend came during the early years of the war when London was under attack by the Nazi Luftwaffe. She was only 19, a young lady whose beauty, charm, and charisma were already gaining notice in high society.

The conflict brought not just damage but also fresh opportunities for people to meet paths in unexpected ways. London's aristocratic circles were teeming with diplomats, officers, and politicians, all seeking sanctuary from the upheaval, but performing the business of war and international politics.

It was at one of these meetings, a dinner party in Mayfair, that Pamela first met Randolph Churchill, the son of the famed Winston Churchill. At the time, Randolph was a rising politician and soldier, having been elected to Parliament at barely 21 and subsequently entering the British Army as a captain in the 4th Queen's Own Hussars. Handsome, with a certain swagger, Randolph was every inch his father's son, albeit not without his defects.

He was notorious for his quick temper, gambling tendencies, and wild lifestyle. But to Pamela, who was attracted to prominent men, Randolph provided a path into the Churchill family—one of Britain's most important and lasting dynasties.

The connection between them was instantaneous, spurred by Randolph's aristocratic heritage and the appeal of his renowned name. Pamela, intrigued by the distinction that comes with being tied to the Churchill heritage, replied with curiosity. The passionate relationship intensified fast. Within weeks of their meeting, Randolph proposed, and Pamela agreed, despite understanding the turbulent character of his personality. Their marriage took place in October 1939, just as the world was plunging into the turmoil of World War II.

The wedding itself was hardly an elaborate ceremony, but it meant Pamela's official admission into the Churchill dynasty. The Churchill family, steeped in history, politics, and military duty, loomed big over British culture.

For Pamela, marrying into this family was a calculated decision that would solidify her place in British nobility and, as she would later prove, prepare her for a life of power on the world stage.

Joining the Churchill Dynasty

Becoming Randolph's wife meant considerably more than simply acquiring the title of Mrs. Churchill; it meant becoming a member of one of Britain's most powerful political families. Winston Churchill, already a towering figure in British politics, had lately been named First Lord of the Admiralty and would shortly become Prime Minister. To marry into this family at such a pivotal juncture in history was, for Pamela, both a pleasure and a responsibility.

Winston, who had watched Randolph go through numerous disastrous relationships, was first dubious of Pamela. However, he rapidly learned to appreciate her composure and intellect. Pamela's capacity to engage with him on political and military subjects delighted the older

Churchill, and over time, she got close to Winston and his wife, Clementine. Pamela, despite her early age, adapted swiftly to the job of being part of a political family. Her charm and diplomatic elegance helped her to negotiate the difficult dynamics of the Churchill family.

Living with the Churchills during the war was no easy feat. The family was always under strain, and Winston's leadership of Britain at its darkest hour meant that their house was frequently the scene of key wartime talks and meetings.

As the wife of Winston's son, Pamela found herself near these momentous times. She listened to debates about military strategy and political negotiations, understanding the nuances of diplomacy and conflict. This setting would establish the framework for her eventual career in politics and diplomacy.

However, the marriage itself was far from blissful. Randolph, whose vices were widely known, proved to be an unstable and unfaithful spouse. His gambling debts escalated, and his drinking frequently led to public tantrums. The conflict simply aggravated his emotional instability.

While Randolph was out fighting in the Middle East, Pamela stayed in London, where she swiftly became one of the most sought-after ladies in society. Her marriage to Randolph, paired with her beauty and brilliance, lifted her social stature to unprecedented heights, providing her access to powerful individuals in both military and diplomatic circles.

During the Blitz, when London was facing the daily horrors of Nazi bombs, Pamela played hostess to an assortment of significant personalities. Her status as a political wife became linked with her developing prominence. She wasn't willing to be a passive spectator; she actively engaged in talks with generals, diplomats, and politicians, developing contacts that would prove essential in her later years.

It was at this period that she started to grasp the art of subtle persuasion, utilizing her charm and wit to gain information and win friends. The Churchill family, for all its grandeur, also had its cracks. Randolph's connection with his father was rocky, defined by furious disagreements and deep-seated anger. Randolph, overwhelmed by the weight of his father's expectations, sometimes lashed out, forcing Pamela to arbitrate between the two.

Despite the stormy nature of their marriage, Pamela remained genuinely committed to Randolph, at least in the early years. She took her role within the Churchill family seriously and sought to preserve the family's reputation in society.

Yet, as the war drew on and Randolph's absences got longer, Pamela found herself more autonomous. She started to develop contacts outside of her marriage, most notably with American diplomats and military officers. Her relations, especially with the rich and important, were not merely personal; they were strategic. Pamela's wartime experiences—hosting meals, meeting with foreign people, and collecting intelligence—would later prove beneficial as she stepped into the realm of American politics.

While her marriage to Randolph finally ended in divorce, it was this phase of her life that started Pamela on the route to being one of the most prominent women of her day.

The Churchill name had given her the platform she needed, but it was her own knowledge, charisma, and drive that enabled her to transcend the position of Randolph's wife. Her experience inside the Churchill clan had honed her political instincts and exposed her to the sophisticated world of diplomacy, war, and global strategy.

Chapter 3: The Seductive Diplomat

When Pamela Churchill, a young aristocrat freshly married into Britain's most prominent family, arrived in Washington, D.C. Throughout World War II, she was thrown into a new and vital role—one that would cement her career as a tough but discreet diplomat.

At barely 20 years old, Pamela had married Randolph Churchill, Winston Churchill's son, but it was her father-in-law who identified her potential as a strategic asset. World War II was raging, and obtaining American backing for Britain was critical to the Allied cause. Winston Churchill realized that the Americans, especially significant political elites and military commanders, had to be kept firmly on the side of the British cause. Pamela, with her beauty, charm, and aristocratic connections, became an unusual but crucial ambassador in these important endeavors.

Pamela's entrée into Washington high society was effortless. Her inherent grace and magnetism attracted some of the most influential men of the day. She became a common presence at dinner parties, cocktail receptions, and events that mingled politics with leisure, soon gaining a reputation as an appealing hostess and conversationalist.

Her presence in Washington was not only cosmetic; Pamela's duty was to win hearts and minds, using her charm and connections to sway

American opinion toward backing Britain's war effort.

It was no secret that Pamela's attraction extended beyond her aristocratic status. She was an engaging communicator, good at putting people at ease, and her beauty and elegance were difficult to ignore. But it was her acute intelligence and awareness of foreign politics that differentiated her from other socialites. She was not merely attending parties; she was strategically placing herself as a crucial influencer in Washington's diplomatic circles.

In the age when official diplomacy was controlled by public relations teams and media scrutiny, personal contacts played a vital role in molding foreign policy. Pamela grasped this well and became a critical bridge between the British and American war operations. She utilized social engagements as chances to meet with powerful Americans, pulling them into her circle. Pamela's approach was both subtle and calculated—while masquerading as a pleasant socialite, she was working assiduously behind the scenes to deepen British-American connections.

Pamela's aptitude for winning over American feelings was especially noticeable in her contacts with significant American men, such as Averell Harriman, the U.S. ambassador to Britain, and Edward R. Murrow, the notable CBS newsman.

Harriman, who would ultimately become her third husband, was originally captivated by Pamela by her beauty but rapidly fell smitten with her knowledge and political understanding.

Their sexual connection was much more than an affair—it was a meeting of minds, with Harriman playing a vital role in helping Pamela traverse the highest echelons of American political life.

Pamela's effect went beyond pillow chat. She was a valued confidante of many major American people, including military officials and members of the U.S. State Department. In her private meetings with them, she argued for increased support for Britain, highlighting the common democratic principles and mutual interests that bonded the two nations.

Pamela was not merely a passive messenger; she was a superb negotiator who knew the delicate balance between persuasion and diplomacy. She articulated the British cause in a manner that appealed to American sensibilities, casting it as a collaborative effort in the struggle for world security and democracy.

In a period when women were generally consigned to the background in political events, Pamela stood out as a woman who exerted significant power, although behind the scenes. Her charm and attractiveness helped her to open doors, but it was her diplomatic skill that enabled her to have a lasting influence.

Pamela's ability to traverse the complicated dynamics of wartime Washington helped consolidate the British-American alliance, a collaboration that would prove critical to the Allies' triumph in World War II.

Wartime Allies: Pamela's Role in World War II Diplomacy

Pamela Churchill's position in World War II diplomacy was one of the best-kept secrets of the period. While the public regarded her as a gorgeous socialite, entertaining politicians and military officials in Washington, she was discreetly functioning as an unofficial ambassador, working relentlessly to build the British-American partnership.

The United States, which had joined the war in 1941, was still adapting to its position as a significant actor on the world stage, and British leaders like Winston Churchill realized that maintaining a tight connection with the U.S. was crucial for the Allied war effort.

Pamela's wartime diplomacy was not performed in official settings but rather in the personal and informal realm of private dinners, exclusive parties, and one-on-one chats. She built ties with key Americans, including military commanders, diplomats, and journalists, using her charm and intellect to advocate for Britain's interests.

Her beauty and elegance made her a sought-after guest at social gatherings, but it was her ability to participate in meaningful political debates that gained her the respect of some of the most prominent men in Washington.

One of Pamela's crucial diplomatic ties at this time was with Edward R. Murrow, the prominent American journalist who had become a household name for his wartime broadcasts from London. Murrow was a personal friend of the

Churchill family, and he and Pamela built a profound bond throughout the war. Pamela frequently exploited her link with Murrow to influence public opinion in the United States, pushing him to underline the significance of the British-American partnership in his broadcasts.

Through her association with Murrow, Pamela was able to mold the narrative of the war in the American media, helping to increase popular support for the Allied effort.

Pamela's bond with Averell Harriman was possibly her most crucial diplomatic partnership throughout the war. As the U.S. ambassador to Britain, Harriman was responsible for coordinating American contributions to the British war effort, and his influence in Washington was substantial. Harriman and

Pamela rapidly grew close, and their sexual bond further reinforced their political collaboration. Harriman, who had a reputation as a strong negotiator, was highly impressed by Pamela's mastery of wartime diplomacy and regularly sought her assistance on problems pertaining to U.S.-British ties.

Their connection became a critical link between the two nations, and Pamela's influence on Harriman helped to guarantee that the United States stayed committed to aiding Britain throughout the war.

In addition to her links with major American leaders, Pamela also played a role in forging personal connections between British and American politicians. She regularly held private meals at the Churchill House in Washington, where British and American ambassadors could gather in an informal environment to discuss the war effort. These meetings, which typically included high-ranking military officers and representatives of the U.S. State Department, gave a rare chance for frank and honest conversations about the difficulties confronting the Allies.

Pamela, who had a flair for making people feel at ease, helped to arrange these meetings, ensuring that the British and American leaders built strong personal ties that would prove important to the success of the Allied war effort.

Pamela's contributions to the war effort remained largely unappreciated during her lifetime, but her effect behind the scenes was unmistakable. She was a skilled diplomat who understood the importance of personal relationships in international politics, and her efforts to strengthen the British-American alliance helped to shape the outcome of World War II.

While she may have been dismissed by some as a mere socialite, Pamela Churchill was, in fact, a powerful force in the world of wartime diplomacy, using her charm, intelligence, and political savvy to win over America's most influential figures and secure their support for Britain's cause.

Chapter 4: Seduction for Victory

During World War II, Pamela Harriman emerged as one of the most unexpected but crucial assets in the diplomatic circles of Washington, D.C. As Winston Churchill's daughter-in-law, she had rare access to both British and American elites. But it was not her position that made her important to the war effort—it was her charm, strategic thinking, and capacity to wield influence via personal connections.

In a period when conventional diplomacy was confined by war and logistics, Pamela perfected the art of informal diplomacy, utilizing social gatherings, dinner parties, and personal contacts to further the British cause.

Pamela's function in diplomatic circles was one of subtle manipulation. Unlike official diplomats, who were restricted by etiquette, she was free to utilize more creative means. She exploited her compelling appearance to amuse and engage senior American leaders, ensuring that the British war effort remained a subject of discourse.

In an era when male diplomats routinely undervalued women, Pamela utilized that error to her advantage. Men perceived her as a delightful friend rather than a strategic player, and it was this same notion that enabled her to acquire important knowledge and change attitudes.

A major part of Pamela's success in Washington was her deep awareness of power relations. She knew that in the high-stakes realm of war, talks over dinner may have just as much weight as those made in official negotiations.

The Roosevelt administration, which was still contemplating the exact scope of its engagement in the war, was a primary target for British attempts to obtain American assistance. Pamela, with her social charm and political understanding, became a crucial conduit of British interests in Washington.

She rapidly attracted powerful persons such as the banker Averell Harriman, who would eventually become her second husband, and Edward R. Murrow, one of America's most trusted newsmen. In these contacts, Pamela identified possibilities to gradually influence perceptions and align American powerbrokers with the British goal. The fundamental essence of her power was predicated on seduction—not just sexual, but intellectual and emotional. She made individuals feel important, listened to, and appreciated, which in turn made them more receptive to her proposals.

Pamela's success in these diplomatic circles also resided in her ability to handle the complicated interplay of personal and political ties. For instance, her connections with guys like Murrow and Harriman were not transactional or superficial; they were founded on mutual respect, appreciation, and shared aims.

Pamela exploited these contacts to acquire access to vital information, frequently before it became public knowledge. In doing so, she played a vital role in collecting information for the British government, her attractiveness hiding the extent of her strategic engagement.

Charm, Secrecy, and Intelligence Gathering in Wartime Washington

Beyond being an informal diplomat, Pamela Harriman was also an asset in information collecting throughout the conflict. Her charm, discretion, and closeness to important persons made her a perfect option for gathering crucial information in a period when every piece of intelligence counted.

Washington during the war was a hotbed of diplomatic activity, and secrets were routinely conveyed in whispers at exclusive parties or private meals. Pamela excelled at this covert style of spying.

Her position in intelligence collecting was never institutionalized, but it was successful. She was privy to critical information supplied by American military officials, politicians, and foreign leaders who frequented the social circles she deftly traversed.

By holding events at her luxurious Georgetown home, Pamela created an atmosphere where guests felt comfortable letting their guard down. As they liked great eating and beautiful discussion, they frequently talked more freely than they may have in more formal circumstances.

One of the important parts of Pamela's intelligence job was her discretion. She understood just when to press for knowledge and when to recede, maintaining a balance between inquiry and trust. Her contacts with individuals like Averell Harriman were not merely amorous but strategic, affording her access to a broad variety of political and military secrets.

Harriman, for example, was extensively engaged in Lend-Lease discussions and other facets of U.S.-British wartime cooperation. Pamela's proximity to him gave the British insight into the direction of U.S. policy and the subtleties of the administration's thinking.

Pamela was equally good at utilizing her beauty and charm to distract from her actual position as an information broker. She played into the caricature of the frivolous socialite while cleverly placing herself into places where she could listen, watch, and extract useful ideas. In many respects, this persona was reminiscent of the traditional female spy cliché, albeit Pamela's techniques were more subtler. She did not need to depend on espionage tactics like cracking codes or intercepting communications; instead, she harnessed the power of conversation and personal connection.

One major illustration of her impact occurred during her friendship with Murrow, who as a journalist had unrivaled access to news, political events, and military strategy.

By building a personal connection with him, Pamela kept herself in the loop regarding the popular feelings and political undercurrents that drove American foreign policy. Additionally, her contact with Averell Harriman not only supplied her with knowledge but also enabled her to plant ideas that may eventually influence his judgments.

Pamela's role in acquiring information goes beyond just overhearing conversations. She had a flair for connecting dots, pulling together fragmentary facts to construct a fuller picture of how events were happening. She would transmit this knowledge back to her friends in London, notably her father-in-law Winston Churchill. In this manner, she was more than simply a socialite; she was a major player in the greater war effort, helping to sway the direction of diplomatic and military policy via her grasp of American thought.

It was in Washington that Pamela refined the abilities that would define her legacy: her capacity to listen, to flatter, to seduce—not only in a romantic sense but in a manner that made others feel important and included. This aptitude for relationship-building, along with her caution and intellect, made her a strong participant in the wartime diplomatic scene. Her competence in these areas enabled her to access and influence talks that impacted the direction of the war, notably in terms of U.S.-British collaboration.

By the time the war ended, Pamela Harriman had acquired a reputation not merely as a lady of charm and beauty but as someone who could tilt the balance of power in subtle but major ways.

Her influence stretched beyond the battlefield, reaching into the highest echelons of diplomatic and military decision-making in Washington. Though she was frequently overlooked by those who regarded her only as a hostess or socialite, her genuine impact was considerably more deep. Through seduction, charm, and an unmatched insight into human psychology, Pamela Harriman had become a vital architect of wartime diplomacy.

Chapter 5: The Fiat Heir

In the post-World War II period, Italy was a nation experiencing enormous upheavals. Amidst the political and economic changes, Pamela Harriman emerged as a crucial participant in remaking European high society. Her impact stretched beyond conventional social engagements; she was essential in defining the narrative and success of some of Europe's most influential personalities.

Pamela Harriman's journey into Italian culture was not only a social visit but a geopolitical one. Upon coming to Rome with her then-husband, she rapidly became a famous figure among the Italian elite. Her charismatic presence, sophisticated elegance, and strategic insight made her a sought-after guest at the grandest of events and a powerful voice in elite circles.

One of the most notable parts of her impact was her friendship with Gianni Agnelli, the successor to the Fiat company. Agnelli was more than simply a rich manufacturer; he was a symbol of Italian strength and elegance, a man who exerted great influence in both industry and society. Pamela Harriman's encounters with Agnelli and his allies were defined by a combination of diplomacy and genuine admiration, which proved to be mutually beneficial.

Harriman's influence in Agnelli's ascent to fame was subtle but important. She helped to expose him to prominent persons and established contacts that were vital for his career. By arranging events and cultivating contacts between Agnelli and other leaders, Harriman played a vital role in consolidating Agnelli's position as a prominent participant on the world scene.

Her influence was not confined to intimate ties; it extended to crafting Agnelli's public image. Through her social networks, Pamela helped to polish Agnelli's image, strengthening his attractiveness and influence inside European circles. She was effective in positioning him as a crucial role in the reconstruction of post-war Europe, both socially and economically.

Harriman's effect was also visible in how she bridged the gap between American and European elites. By utilizing her American contacts, she was able to organize economic agreements and political alliances that were good for Agnelli and Fiat. Her ability to negotiate these complicated social and political settings made her an important partner to Agnelli and a significant figure in European society.

The Rise of Agnelli: Italy's 'Uncrowned King' on the Global Stage

Gianni Agnelli, sometimes referred to as Italy's 'uncrowned king,' was a man whose power reached well beyond the boardrooms of Fiat. His ascent to prominence was not just a product of his inheritance but also a monument to his strategic vision and the strategic contacts he developed, many of which were helped by Pamela Harriman.

Agnelli's elevation in the global arena was defined by his ability to negotiate and influence numerous industries. As the CEO of Fiat, he turned the corporation from a post-war industrial powerhouse into a symbol of Italian ingenuity and elegance.

His leadership was characterized by a combination of conventional commercial acumen with a new approach to company strategy. Agnelli was essential in pushing Fiat into new markets and growing its power, not only inside Italy but abroad.

Pamela Harriman's effect on Agnelli's ascent may be related to three significant reasons. Firstly, her social aptitude and diplomatic talents enabled Agnelli to create critical contacts with other powerful persons. Through her, Agnelli acquired access to a network of politicians, businesspeople, and cultural icons, which proved vital for Fiat's development and his personal brand.

One significant example of this impact was Harriman's involvement in helping Agnelli's entrance into the American market. Her contacts and reputation allowed her to introduce Agnelli to important leaders in the U.S., unlocking doors that were previously blocked to foreign investors. This access was vital in helping Fiat establish a presence in one of the world's most competitive marketplaces.

Furthermore, Pamela's strategic placement of Agnelli inside European high society had a crucial part in boosting his worldwide image. By linking him with significant cultural and political personalities, she sought to raise Agnelli's position from a rich entrepreneur to a renowned worldwide leader. Her ability to control public opinion and build a sophisticated image for Agnelli was a critical aspect of his ascension.

Agnelli's prominence as a cultural and social symbol was also a consequence of Harriman's influence. She managed to position him as a symbol of Italian elegance and modernism, attributes that resonated with foreign audiences. This picture was significant in consolidating Fiat's brand and in making Agnelli a major role in worldwide talks on industry and culture.

The development of Gianni Agnelli was also defined by his engagement in numerous international organizations and his position as a mediator in European affairs. Pamela Harriman's impact was clear in how she helped Agnelli traverse these difficult international settings. Her ability to give strategic advice and make vital contacts was essential in Agnelli's success in these fields.

Chapter 6: A Continental Affair

Pamela Harriman's life was a complex tapestry of influence, passion, and strategic relationships, all of which played a key part in developing her incredible power. Her relationships, frequently sensationalized, were more than just personal excursions; they were crucial in extending her authority and solidifying her standing on the world scene.

These partnerships were not only about personal fulfillment but were carefully choreographed movements in a bigger game of political and social manipulation. One of Pamela's most noteworthy partnerships was with the Italian entrepreneur Gianni Agnelli. The Fiat heir was more than a rich businessman; he was a prominent actor in European politics and high society. Pamela's link with Agnelli was a strategic partnership that enabled her to achieve admission into the highest echelons of European power.

Their connection, distinguished by a combination of real devotion and calculated calculation, enabled Pamela to utilize Agnelli's position to achieve her own political goals. Agnelli's assistance was important in raising her voice in European circles, where she utilized her charm and contacts to convince key leaders and win vital relationships.

Pamela's escapades also included a well-publicized liaison with the prominent socialite and diplomat, Aly Khan. This partnership further reinforced her status as a strong social and political force. Aly Khan, a member of the famed Pakistani royal family, was not only significant in his own right but also a bridge to other high-profile relationships throughout Europe and the Middle East.

Through her association with Khan, Pamela got access to a network of prominent persons, improving her stature and capacity to influence world affairs.

These romances were not casual flings but strategic collaborations that gave Pamela crucial access to the world's most powerful and influential persons. Her ability to negotiate these high-stakes issues with elegance and precision was a credit to her competence in the art of diplomacy and influence. Each engagement, although personal in character, was also a well-planned move aimed to reinforce her position and achieve her strategic aims.

The World of Fashion, Politics, and Wealth: The Life of a Jetsetter

Pamela Harriman's jet-setting lifestyle was more than a reflection of her social position; it was a deliberate weapon that enabled her to retain and increase her influence across continents. Her life was a seamless combination of fashion, politics, and riches, and she maneuvered this world with a finesse that fascinated everyone around her.

Fashion plays a key influence on Pamela's public character. Her exquisite style and choice of clothes were not merely questions of personal taste but purposeful judgments that reinforced her image as a smart and prominent personality.

Her attire, meticulously picked by some of the world's greatest designers, was a statement of her position and a technique for gaining media attention. Each dress was selected to portray an image of elegance and authority, ensuring that she stayed in the public eye and at the heart of social and political discourse.

Pamela's engagement in high society gatherings was another major component of her jet-setting existence. From dazzling parties in Paris to private gatherings in London, she was a permanent presence at the world's most renowned social engagements.

These gatherings presented her with excellent opportunity to network with key persons and affect public image. Her participation at these parties was not only about socializing but also about creating and keeping contacts that were vital to her political and social power.

Wealth and extravagance were crucial to Pamela's lifestyle, allowing her to glide seamlessly through the highest circles of society. Her access to great financial means enabled her to hold expensive parties, sponsor political organizations, and maintain a lifestyle that kept her in the limelight. This money was not simply a symbol of achievement but an actual instrument that permitted her continuous influence and power.

In addition to fashion and riches, Pamela's ability to manage the intricate realm of politics was a distinguishing characteristic of her jet-setting existence. Her excursions were not simply about relaxation but were meticulously organized to maximize her effect and influence. Whether attending international conferences or private encounters with world leaders, Pamela exploited these chances to further her interests and impact global events.

Her existence as a jetsetter was distinguished by a continual interaction between personal and professional domains. The connections she built, the fashion choices she made, and the cash she possessed were all components of a well-organized strategy aimed at maximizing her power and influence.

Pamela's ability to smoothly combine these pieces into a unified and appealing story was a credit to her expertise and strategic insight.

Chapter 7: The Move to America

When Pamela Harriman made her move to America in the early 1970s, it was not merely a physical transfer but a major makeover of her public character and impact. Having previously lived a life steeped in European nobility and political intrigue, Pamela's entrée into American high society forced her to build a new persona from the ground up, one that resonated with a distinct social and political context.

Pamela's shift was defined by her methodical strategy to re-establish herself among America's elite. The first stage in this procedure was getting a conspicuous house in New York, the hub of American high society. She and her husband, Averell Harriman, picked a magnificent apartment on Park Avenue, a symbol of both luxury and prominence. The Harriman name, along with Pamela's European heritage, rapidly put them at the forefront of New York's social scene.

Pamela's ability to traverse the complexity of American social hierarchies was built on her thorough awareness of the power dynamics inside elite circles. She embraced her new post with the same subtlety that had distinguished her diplomatic undertakings in Europe.

Through a succession of well-organized social events—lavish parties, exclusive dinners, and high-profile charity galas—Pamela relaunched herself as a cultured and important woman. Her charisma and sophisticated manner were important tools, helping her to forge contacts with significant persons across numerous professions.

Her social approach involves associating oneself with crucial persons who might boost her stature. Pamela built contacts with notable media moguls, philanthropists, and political officials. Her ties with people such as Barbara Walters, Gloria Steinem, and Frank Sinatra were not only social but purposeful, placing her as a major presence in American elite circles. This network not only boosted her social position but also gave outlets for her to have influence on political and cultural concerns.

Pamela's transformation also included conforming to American conventions while preserving her particular European flare. She mixed American informality with European elegance, producing a distinctive appearance that was both friendly and dignified. This mix of styles helped her negotiate the American social milieu and made her a popular character in elite social occasions.

Navigating the World of New York's Elite

Once Pamela Harriman had successfully re-established herself in high society, she proceeded to utilize her position to influence American politics and culture. New York City, with its dynamic social and political activity, offered a fertile ground for her to construct a web of influence that reached well beyond conventional social contact.

Pamela's absorption into New York's elite was defined by her strategic engagement in significant social and charity events. Her engagement in charitable work, notably via organizations such as the Metropolitan Museum of Art and numerous cultural institutions, helped her to solidify her position among the city's most important socialites.

By advocating causes that were both respectable and politically important, Pamela established her position as a person of importance in American high society.

Navigating the world of New York's elite needed more than just social elegance; it demanded a sophisticated awareness of the city's political terrain. Pamela leveraged her broad network to connect with political leaders and activists, extending her influence in American political circles. Her ability to connect with folks across the political spectrum made her a great asset to both the Democratic and Republican parties. Her support for numerous political movements, along with her smart endorsements, helped shape political discourse and influence critical choices.

Pamela's significance in molding public opinion was further increased by her appearance in the media. She became a regular guest on talk programs and was published in popular periodicals, which helped maintain her profile and enhance her impact.

Her clear and perceptive criticism of political and social problems positioned her as a thought leader, helping her to affect public opinion and further establish her place in the elite.

One of the most crucial features of Pamela's navigation of New York's elite was her participation in the political revival of the Democratic Party.

Her intimate ties with people such as Bill Clinton enabled her to exercise great influence over the party's direction and tactics. By using her social connections and political savvy, Pamela played a significant role in rejuvenating the Democratic Party and supporting its candidates.

Chapter 8: Rebuilding the Democratic Party

Pamela Harriman's transformation from a dazzling socialite to a significant participant in American politics was a stunning regeneration. After decades spent creating European high society and working behind the scenes to influence world politics, Harriman turned her focus to rejuvenating the American Democratic Party, a mission that would redefine her reputation in the U.S. political arena.

Her political rebirth was not a simple random event but the product of planned maneuvers and a well-timed alignment with the interests of the Democratic Party. By the late 1970s and early 1980s, the Democratic Party was in disarray. The party having lost the presidential election to Richard Nixon in 1972, experienced significant internal divides, and struggled to portray a unified front. Harriman, with her broad network and political skill, saw a chance to employ her substantial influence to assist the party recover its footing.

Arriving in New York with a reputation founded on both charm and effectiveness, Pamela Harriman started to work behind the scenes to develop contacts with important Democrats.

Her intimate contacts with important people, like Senator Daniel Patrick Moynihan and Governor Mario Cuomo, enabled her to use her influence and resources in favor of the party's resurrection. Harriman's engagement in fundraising activities was especially remarkable. She was essential in planning high-profile events that not only garnered major financial support for the party but also helped repair its image and legitimacy.

One of the important moments in her political rebirth occurred when she organized a series of prominent dinners and receptions, intentionally inviting possible contributors, political heavyweights, and media people.

These meetings were more than just social affairs; they were chances for Harriman to quietly direct the talks and establish partnerships that would be vital for the party's future success. Her ability to bring together diverse groups within the party and establish a feeling of togetherness was vital during this era of restoration.

The Democratic National Committee and Her Role Behind the Scenes

Pamela Harriman's participation in the Democratic National Committee (DNC) was essential but largely overlooked by the public. While she never had an official position inside the DNC, her effect was enormous. She acted as a behind-the-scenes power broker, leveraging her wide network and political knowledge to mold the party's plans and choices.

One of her significant contributions was in the field of fundraising. The Democratic Party has suffered from financial instability and was in severe need of resources to fight successfully against the Republicans. Harriman's fundraising efforts were nothing short of transformational. She delved into her broad network of affluent contributors, using her contacts to get big donations. Her ability to recruit high-profile contributors was important in restocking the party's coffers and guaranteeing its financial stability.

Harriman's impact went beyond money. She was a strategic counselor to party leaders, giving insights and recommendations on critical political tactics and choices. Her background in European politics gave her a distinct viewpoint that proved beneficial to American political strategists. She was especially effective at understanding and managing the subtleties of electoral politics, which was vital as the party worked to repair its image and recover public confidence.

One of the significant successes during her time working with the DNC was her involvement in the 1982 midterm elections. Harriman played a vital role in organizing and directing the party's operations, ensuring that resources were adequately distributed and that important contests were carefully targeted. Her behind-the-scenes labor contributed greatly to the party's triumph in these elections, helping to pave the path for future successes.

Harriman's influence also extended to crafting the party's platform and programs. While she did not actively design policy, her thoughts and viewpoints contributed to determining the party's course.

She worked extensively with senior party members to ensure that the Democratic platform addressed crucial concerns and connected with people. Her strategic assistance was important in helping the party negotiate the complicated political terrain of the 1980s.

Throughout her tenure with the DNC, Pamela Harriman kept a low profile, preferring to work quietly and behind the scenes. Her impact was felt via the outcomes of her work rather than through public plaudits. The influence of her efforts was visible in the revival of the Democratic Party, which gradually started to reclaim its power and place in American politics.

Harriman's achievements were not without hurdles. She experienced pushback from individuals who were distrustful of her goals and techniques. Some considered her as an outsider or a remnant of a bygone period, while others questioned her dedication to the Democratic cause. However, Harriman's ability to manage these hurdles and accomplish actual outcomes revealed her passion and efficacy.

By the late 1980s, the Democratic Party had begun to show indications of rebirth. The foundation created by Pamela Harriman and others who worked behind the scenes helped to revive the party and set the basis for future achievements. Her contribution to this process, although not always obvious, was vital in ensuring that the Democratic Party emerged from a period of collapse and started to regain its power and importance.

Chapter 9: Spotlighting Bill Clinton

By the late 1980s, the American Democratic Party was in disarray. After losing the president in 1984 and confronting a divided political environment, it was evident that a fresh, creative leader was required to rejuvenate the party and launch a credible fight against the Republicans. This was a period ripe for political intervention, and Pamela Harriman, with her sharp political instincts and unequaled network, recognized an opportunity.

Harriman's debut in U.S. politics was defined by her ability to negotiate high society and political hallways with ease. Her impact was not just a product of her social rank but of her strategic vision. Recognizing the need for a compelling leader who could bridge the gap between conventional Democratic beliefs and a new, more inclusive vision, she turned her focus to an unassuming governor from Arkansas.

Bill Clinton was a relatively obscure person on the national scene in 1988. He was the governor of a tiny southern state, with modest achievements and minimal national notoriety.

However, Harriman recognized possibilities in Clinton's ability to connect with the common American and his skilled approach to governing. His bid for re-election as governor in 1986 had proved his political skill and ability to rally people, characteristics that Harriman thought were needed for a successful national campaign.

Harriman, exploiting her huge political network, started to secretly advocate Clinton within Democratic circles. She presented him to key persons and possible funders, highlighting his abilities and potential.

Her endorsement was not only a show of support; it was a planned effort to enhance Clinton's reputation and garner essential backing. This behind-the-scenes work was important in presenting Clinton as a potential contender for higher office.

Her method encompassed more than simply political endorsements; it was about establishing a story. Harriman's backing helped construct a compelling picture of a leader who was not just a successful governor but also a visionary who could revive the Democratic Party. This storyline was vital in transforming the view of Clinton from a regional figure to a national candidate.

Vaulting a Political Unknown to National Power

The 1992 presidential election was a turning moment for the Democratic Party, and Pamela Harriman's participation in Clinton's ascension to power was vital. By the time Clinton formally launched his campaign, he was still regarded as an outsider with a hard path ahead. However, Harriman's groundwork had created the platform for his climb.

Clinton's campaign was originally hampered by obstacles. He faced criticism from established political elites, media scrutiny, and a wide field of Democratic competitors. Yet, Harriman's influence helped lessen these barriers. Her endorsement gave Clinton a degree of legitimacy and support that was needed to gain momentum.

One of the important parts of Harriman's approach was her concentration on fundraising. She utilized her contacts with affluent donors and powerful personalities to win significant financial assistance for Clinton's campaign. This financial backing enabled Clinton to establish a solid campaign infrastructure, engage in significant advertising, and reach voters throughout the nation.

Harriman's effect went beyond financial help. She had a significant role in developing Clinton's campaign strategy. Her insights into political dynamics and voter behavior helped improve Clinton's campaign and concentrate on critical themes. Under her supervision, Clinton's campaign highlighted themes of economic regeneration, healthcare reform, and a fresh approach to governing, connecting with a wide public.

Moreover, Harriman provided Clinton access to prominent political people and media celebrities. These relationships were important in improving Clinton's visibility and reputation. Her ability to open doors and generate chances for Clinton was a credit to her strategic aptitude and political insight.

As the primary season continued, Clinton's campaign gathered momentum. His performances in debates, along with a rising public support base, drove him to the forefront of the Democratic field. Harriman's behind-the-scenes efforts were important in negotiating the obstacles of the primaries and obtaining Clinton's candidacy.

The general election brought a fresh set of issues, with the incumbent President George H. W. Bush enjoying high popularity ratings and a solid economic performance. However, Clinton's campaign, boosted by Harriman's strategic ideas and backing, focused on contrasting Clinton's vision for the future with the perceived stagnation of the Bush government. Key concerns such as the economy, healthcare, and a new approach to governing were fundamental to Clinton's campaign theme.

Harriman's influence lasted into the general election. Her contacts with powerful leaders, media personalities, and contributors gave Clinton the resources and exposure required to compete successfully. Her strategic guidance helped Clinton manage the challenges of a national campaign and handle crucial concerns with clarity.

On election day, Clinton's campaign succeeded in securing the White House. His win was not simply a personal triumph but also a monument to Harriman's strategic vision and political savvy. Her involvement in hand-picking Clinton and directing his ascension to national power was a masterpiece in political strategy and persuasion.

Clinton's presidency represented a new era for the Democratic Party and American politics. His ideas and leadership were formed by the foundations created during his campaign, with Harriman's influence being a crucial component in his ascension to power. Her contributions to Clinton's achievement were a mirror of her greater effect on U.S. politics, displaying her capacity to change political destiny from behind the scenes.

Chapter 10: The Appointment to Ambassador

Pamela Harriman's selection as Ambassador to France in 1993 was the product of decades of strategic maneuvering, political skill, and persistent charm. This appointment was not just a product of her social status but also a testimonial to her exceptional influence and ability to negotiate the convoluted field of international diplomacy.

The route to this prominent job started even before Harriman's official appointment. Her initial journey into American politics had been distinguished by her successful attempts to revive the Democratic Party in the early 1980s.

Her strategic skill was obvious in her ability to propel Bill Clinton to national prominence. Clinton's subsequent triumph in the 1992 presidential election was, in part, a reflection of Harriman's behind-the-scenes influence.

By the time Clinton was elected, Pamela Harriman was already acknowledged as a powerful influence in American political circles. Her participation in the Democratic rebirth and her intimate contacts with prominent persons made her a great contender for a high-profile diplomatic appointment.

The ambassadorship to France was not only an honor; it was a strategic decision by the Clinton administration to use her special abilities in the world arena. The choice of Harriman for this job was a masterstroke in diplomatic strategy.

France was an important ally, and the relationship between the U.S. and France was experiencing a time of reevaluation. The appointment was aimed to improve connections and add a new perspective to U.S.-French relations. Harriman's broad network, proven diplomatic talents, and profound awareness of international politics made her the perfect choice to manage these difficult connections.

The appointment process itself was a meticulously choreographed event. Clinton's staff grasped the importance of this post and the influence it would have on his administration's foreign policy. They knew that Harriman's appointment would not only reinforce relations with France but also convey a strong image of competence and intelligence. This choice showed Clinton's commitment to using experienced and skilled personnel to advocate American interests overseas.

Pamela's Preparation for France

Once appointed, Pamela Harriman's preparation for her job as Ambassador to France was comprehensive and careful. Her approach was representative of her strategic attitude and her devotion to mastering the complexities of her new role.

Understanding the Diplomatic Landscape: Pamela Harriman understood that the role of an ambassador was not just about representing her country but also about navigating complex political landscapes. Before her formal job, she immersed herself in the subtleties of U.S.-French relations. She researched the present political atmosphere in France, the important actors in

French politics, and the historical backdrop of the bilateral relationship.

Harriman's preparation entailed intensive briefings with State Department officials, intelligence professionals, and political analysts. These briefings presented her with a full picture of France's political dynamics, economic status, and important areas of importance for both nations. She also sought views from past ambassadors and diplomats who had served in France, garnering useful perspectives on the problems and possibilities she would encounter.

Building Relationships: One of Harriman's talents was her ability to develop and keep connections. Before she departed for Paris, she exploited her broad network to develop ties with key French people. She reached out to major political figures, corporate executives, and cultural icons to establish the framework for her reign. Harriman's reputation as a talented diplomat and her charm played a vital influence in these exchanges.

In addition to cultivating links with French contacts, Harriman also concentrated on expanding her ties with the American expatriate population in France. These relationships would be essential in supporting her diplomatic efforts and offering insights into the local climate.

Her connections with this population helped her understand the needs and problems of American citizens living overseas, which would be a key component of her work as ambassador.

Cultural and Linguistic Preparation: Recognizing the need for cultural sensitivity in diplomacy, Pamela Harriman made major efforts to acquaint herself with French culture and language. Although she was already competent in French, she participated in extensive language instruction to develop her abilities and guarantee that she could speak successfully in all circumstances.

Harriman's cultural preparation includes learning French traditions, etiquette, and social conventions. She sought assistance from cultural specialists and participated in talks with friends and coworkers who had lived in France. This training was vital for negotiating the complexities of French social relations and ensuring that she could represent American interests with respect and understanding.

Setting Diplomatic Objectives: Before her departure, Pamela Harriman worked closely with President Clinton and his staff to identify her diplomatic goals. They identified important goals for her term, including improving economic relations between the U.S. and France, tackling international security challenges, and encouraging cultural interchange.

Harriman's aims were matched with the wider goals of the Clinton administration, which intended to expand U.S.-French collaboration in several sectors. Her mission was to organize negotiations on economic agreements, work on security measures, and develop mutual understanding between the two countries. She was also entrusted with promoting American principles and interests in a manner that connected with French people.

Personal and Public Image: Pamela Harriman's public image was a key component of her preparation. Her status as a dazzling socialite and important woman was both a benefit and a hindrance. She needed to blend her public image with the demands of her official position.

To combat this, Harriman worked with public relations specialists to construct a carefully controlled image that stressed her diplomatic competence and dedication to American interests. She prepared for her public appearances by rehearsing essential topics and focused on how to portray herself as a serious and effective ambassador of the United States.

Chapter 11: Charm and Diplomacy in Paris

When Pamela Harriman was named Ambassador to France in 1993, she was heading into a post that needed not just diplomatic skill but also a delicate touch in negotiating the complicated political and social terrain of one of America's longest friends. Her selection was welcomed with a combination of skepticism and excitement; some questioned her qualifications for such an important post, while others hoped her unique mixture of charm and strategic acumen might bridge divides between the U.S. and France.

France, with its rich cultural past and complicated political atmosphere, posed a unique set of obstacles for Harriman. The early 1990s were a time of tremendous change for France, with the nation coping with economic challenges, a shifting political environment, and a changing relationship with the United States.

The presidency of François Mitterrand was coming to an end, and the political environment was being changed as new leaders and ideas arose. Against this background, Harriman had to negotiate a political scene defined by both familiarity and change.

Harriman's attitude was classically diplomatic. She knew that to be successful in her post, she needed to establish ties with a broad variety of political players, from the retiring Mitterrand to the incoming President Jacques Chirac. This requires a careful mix of expressing respect for

French political traditions while yet promoting American interests. Harriman's plan comprised a blend of personal appeal and professional expertise. She hosted a succession of high-profile events and state dinners, where her skilled talks and genuine interest in French culture served to endear her to powerful persons.

Her charm was not only a personal attribute but a strategic instrument in her diplomatic armory. Harriman utilized it to create relationships with French authorities and to promote a spirit of goodwill between the two countries.

Her ability to speak French fluently and her strong respect for French art and culture helped her to connect with the French elite on a personal level. This link was critical in a nation where personal contacts frequently play a major role in political talks.

One of the primary obstacles Harriman faced was the doubt about her capacity to represent U.S. interests successfully. Many in France considered her as a political outsider, an image she tried hard to change. She attended countless political and social gatherings, interacting with French lawmakers, business executives, and cultural celebrities.

Her presence was a daily reminder of the U.S. commitment to preserving a strong relationship with France, and her attempts to connect with French society on its terms served to dispel questions about her credentials.

In addition to her social obligations, Harriman also had to handle some important political matters. One of the key worries was the emerging European Union and its influence on transatlantic ties.

The 1990s witnessed important advancements in European integration, notably the Maastricht Treaty and the adoption of the euro. France was at the vanguard of these developments, and Harriman wanted to guarantee that U.S. interests were recognized in the larger framework of European integration.

Harriman's ability to handle these problems was credited to her diplomatic talent and awareness of the intricate interaction of politics, culture, and personal connections. She managed to combine the frequently contradictory objectives of American foreign policy with the need to maintain good and respectful ties with her French colleagues.

Repairing Transatlantic Relations

One of Harriman's key aims as Ambassador to France was to rebuild and enhance the transatlantic friendship between the United States and France. The early 1990s were a time of tense relations between the two countries, driven by disputes on numerous critical topics, including trade, military, and foreign policy.

The end of the Cold War has led to a re-evaluation of global alliances and a change in the worldwide balance of power. France, under Mitterrand and then Chirac, was negotiating a new position in a world where the U.S. was rising as the single superpower. This move produced conflict between the two states, as France attempted to impose its power in a shifting global order.

Harriman tackled the mission of restoring transatlantic ties with a firm appreciation of the significance of communication and collaboration. Her technique was to concentrate on areas of common interest and to resolve sources of dispute via direct and constructive involvement. One of her primary goals was to promote high-level talks between American and French officials to address common challenges and to identify chances for cooperation.

Her attempts to mend the relationship were not confined to political conversations. Harriman also recognized the role of cultural diplomacy in developing connections between the two countries. She planned a series of cultural exchanges and activities that emphasized the common values and interests of the U.S. and France.

These activities comprised art exhibits, music performances, and educational programs that brought together American and French artists, researchers, and students. By highlighting the cultural ties between the two nations, Harriman was able to build a spirit of mutual regard and understanding.

In addition to her artistic activities, Harriman was actively engaged in tackling particular political and economic concerns that were producing tension between the U.S. and France. One of the key areas of concern was commerce. The 1990s witnessed several trade conflicts between the two countries, including tensions over agricultural subsidies and market access. Harriman worked extensively with French authorities to negotiate answers to these concerns, stressing the need for fair and free commerce in sustaining a strong transatlantic connection.

Another key area of concern for Harriman was defense and security. The end of the Cold War had led to a re-evaluation of military objectives and alliances, and the U.S. and France had divergent views on the future of NATO and other security arrangements.

Harriman's diplomatic efforts were aimed at establishing common ground on these problems and ensuring that both countries could work together successfully in solving global security difficulties.

Harriman's approach to restoring transatlantic ties was marked by her ability to balance charm with substance. She utilized her personal contacts and diplomatic talents to generate trust and create a pleasant environment for discussions. Her efforts were crucial in overcoming the barriers that had strained the U.S.-France relationship and in establishing the framework for a more cooperative and productive alliance.

Chapter 12: Bosnia and the Peak of American Power

The Bosnian war of the 1990s was a complicated and terrible episode in European history. Emerging from the fall of Yugoslavia, it was defined by ethnic unrest, brutality, and a humanitarian catastrophe that grabbed the world's attention.

Amidst this turbulence, the United States found itself at the vanguard of diplomatic attempts to broker peace, a position that mirrored its expanding global power after the Cold War. The background of this diplomatic attempt was a changing environment of power and influence, with the U.S. negotiating a careful path between involvement and restraint.

The United States' engagement in the Bosnian war was inspired by a mix of moral responsibility, geopolitical strategy, and the need to calm a dangerous area. The Clinton administration, in particular, was under great pressure to intervene as the international community battled with how to handle the ethnic cleansing and crimes that were occurring. The U.S. strategy was multi-faceted, comprising economic penalties, diplomatic discussions, and, eventually, military action via NATO.

At the foundation of the American diplomatic policy was the need to establish a consensus among foreign partners, handle the intricacies of the Balkan issue, and meet the conflicting interests of many parties. The U.S. worked closely with the European Union, the United

Nations, and regional countries to establish a cohesive strategy that intended to stop the bloodshed and bring about a durable peace. This involves high-stakes talks, shuttle diplomacy, and the balancing of national objectives with humanitarian aspirations.

The Dayton Peace Accords, signed in December 1995, were the conclusion of these efforts. The accords, reached in Dayton, Ohio, represented a crucial milestone in the struggle and were essential in putting an end to the war.

The achievement of the agreements was a credit to the smart diplomacy and strategic maneuvering of U.S. officials, who negotiated a complicated web of regional and international influences to create a shaky peace.

Pamela's Role in the Bosnian Peace Process

Pamela Harriman's engagement in the Bosnian peace process demonstrated her unique position as a diplomatic force and strategic influencer. As the U.S. Ambassador to France, her position expanded beyond typical diplomatic tasks, utilizing her personal contacts and political ability to influence international discussions and impact the conclusion of the war.

Harriman's contribution to the Bosnian peace process was marked by her ability to handle the nuances of international diplomacy with grace. Her knowledge and contacts played a vital role in fostering communication amongst the many parties participating in the discussions. She was skilled at leveraging her charm and political intelligence to create connections with important players, including European leaders and U.S. officials, who were vital to the peace effort.

One of Harriman's key achievements was her role in the diplomatic activities leading up to the Dayton discussions. She worked closely with Richard Holbrooke, the U.S. Special Envoy for Bosnia, and other important negotiators to guarantee that the peace negotiations continued successfully.

Her function was not only about direct negotiating but also about supporting the broader strategy, maintaining connections, and ensuring that the U.S. viewpoint was well-represented.

Harriman's influence extended to her relationships with French President Jacques Chirac and other European politicians. Her diplomatic talents and her ability to portray a unified front were essential in securing support for the U.S. and NATO's approach to the fight.

She leveraged her position to urge for a strong international reaction, pressing for increased European engagement and ensuring that the peace process gained the required support from key nations.

In addition to her professional diplomatic responsibilities, Harriman's connections and reputation played a role in smoothing diplomatic barriers. Her vast network of relationships across political and social circles gave significant information and aided behind-the-scenes discussions. Her attendance at crucial events and her contact with significant persons served to reinforce the international coalition's efforts and contributed to the ultimate success of the peace process.

The Dayton Accords, which marked the conclusion of the Bosnian war, were a monument to the combined efforts of diplomats, notably Pamela Harriman. The agreements provided the basis for peace in Bosnia and set the way for the country's restoration and reconciliation.

Harriman's engagement in this process demonstrated her ability to merge personal diplomacy with high-stakes talks, showing her contributions to one of the most major diplomatic triumphs of the 1990s.

Harriman's engagement in the Bosnian peace process was not only about her function as an ambassador but also about her larger effect on American and world diplomacy. Her actions were a reflection of her greater dedication to global stability and her capacity to influence critical outcomes in complicated international circumstances.

Chapter 13: Friends, Foes, and Lovers

Pamela Harriman's life was a magnificent tapestry woven with the threads of some of the most powerful and colorful characters of the 20th century. Her social circle was not only a collection of prominent persons; it was a network that spanned countries and held great influence.

From the Kennedys to Truman Capote, Aly Khan to Frank Sinatra, Harriman's associations were essential in molding both her fate and the larger political environment. This section looks into her relationships with these major personalities, illustrating how she impacted and was inspired by them.

The Kennedys

Pamela Harriman's connection with the Kennedy family was one of mutual admiration and strategic partnership. Her first substantial engagement with the Kennedys started in the early 1960s when she played a vital role in obtaining support for John F. Kennedy's presidential campaign.

Pamela's charm and social savvy were important in forging a connection between the Kennedy campaign and key funders and political players.

Pamela's bond with Jacqueline Kennedy was especially significant. The two ladies, both beacons of elegance and grace, established a kinship that transcended beyond social pleasantries. Pamela appreciated Jacqueline's composure and knowledge, while Jacqueline treasured Pamela's political views and connections. Their connection was symbolic of Pamela's ability to negotiate the top tiers of society with ease and competence.

This partnership also opened doors for Pamela in Washington, permitting her further engagement in high-profile political and diplomatic capacities.

The friendship with the Kennedy family continued to thrive following JFK's killing. Pamela's social skills and political instincts were once again called upon as she worked to help Robert Kennedy's Senate candidacy. The Kennedy family's backing and assistance were vital in Pamela's ascension inside the Democratic Party. Her ability to integrate her social acumen with political strategy made her a vital partner to the Kennedys, and her influence was noticed in the circles that counted most.

Truman Capote

Truman Capote, the famed writer and socialite, was one of Pamela Harriman's closest and most colorful acquaintances. Their relationship was distinguished by mutual admiration and a shared appreciation for the better things in life. Capote's exuberant personality and keen wit matched Pamela's charm and refinement.

Pamela's social events regularly featured Capote, and their interactions were a combination of high drama and real fondness. Capote's observations and insights into the social and political environment were important to Pamela, giving her a unique perspective on the power systems she traversed. In exchange, Pamela's contacts and influence were important in advancing Capote's writing career. Their connection was a monument to Pamela's ability to establish relationships with a varied spectrum of personalities, each adding to her impact and success.

Aly Khan

Aly Khan, the son of the Aga Khan and a renowned social figure, was another major influence in Pamela Harriman's life. Their partnership was a combination of personal and political interests, demonstrating Pamela's aptitude for managing complicated social interactions. Aly Khan was recognized for his riches, charisma, and connections throughout Europe and the Middle East, making him a vital partner in Pamela's political and social pursuits.

Pamela's friendship with Aly Khan also had a considerable influence on her European contacts. Through Khan, Pamela was exposed to a larger group of powerful European personalities, strengthening her social and political stature.

Their encounters were marked by mutual respect and strategic cooperation, as each attempted to use their relationships for their interests. Pamela's ability to sustain a connection with Aly Khan showcased her diplomatic talents and her penchant for forging partnerships that expanded her power across multiple domains.

Frank Sinatra

Frank Sinatra, the famed singer and actor, was another significant player in Pamela Harriman's social circle. Their connection was both personal and professional, with Pamela regularly attending Sinatra's concerts and social occasions. Sinatra's charm and charisma were well-matched with Pamela's social ability, and their interactions were a combination of mutual adoration and strategic cooperation.

Sinatra's prominence in the entertainment business and his ties with important persons supplied Pamela with more channels of influence. Their connection enabled Pamela to get into the entertainment world's network, which proved useful in her political and social pursuits.

Sinatra's support and companionship were crucial throughout critical stages in Pamela's career, and their friendship highlighted her ability to combine personal and professional ties smoothly.

Pamela Harriman's social circle grew beyond the Kennedys, Capote, Khan, and Sinatra to include a varied variety of notable personalities. Her interactions with high-profile persons such as Gloria Steinem, Ed Murrow, and Kay Graham were crucial in developing her career and spreading her impact.

Gloria Steinem, the famed feminist and writer, was a friend and ally who shared Pamela's dedication to social change. Their partnership was distinguished by a mutual regard for each other's work and a shared goal for social advancement. Pamela's commitment to feminist issues was reinforced and accentuated by her friendship with Steinem, and their cooperation on different projects emphasized Pamela's ability to link herself with significant social movements.

Ed Murrow, the acclaimed broadcaster, was another significant player in Pamela's network. Murrow's work in journalism and his reputation for ethics and professionalism matched Pamela's efforts in diplomacy and politics. Their encounters generally revolved around talks of current events and the role of media in affecting public opinion. Pamela's relationships with Murrow provided her with vital insights into media dynamics and strengthened her ability to maneuver the political terrain efficiently.

Kay Graham, the publisher of The Washington Post, was another significant friend who played a vital part in Pamela's career. Graham's backing and endorsement were essential in increasing Pamela's reputation in political and social circles. Their connection was defined by a mutual knowledge of the power of media and its influence on public perception. Pamela's friendship with Graham demonstrated her capacity to form relationships with prominent players in the media and publishing business.

Chapter 14: The Final Chapter: Power till the End

Pamela Harriman, who astonished the world with her attractiveness, political intelligence, and social connections, continued to exercise influence and make a lasting effect until the end of her life. Her senior years were distinguished by a combination of ongoing political participation, public service, and the subtle, lasting force that defined her career.

Pamela's Later Years

After her historic term as U.S. Ambassador to France, Pamela Harriman went into a more private but significant post. The early 1990s was a moment of consolidation and introspection for

Harriman, who had done much yet remained passionately involved in public life. Her accomplishments at this period were not as high-profile as her previous triumphs, but they were no less vital.

Return to Private Life

In the years after her ambassadorship, Pamela Harriman returned to a more private realm. However, her impact did not decrease. She spent substantial time at her residences in Paris and the United States, where she continued to connect with prominent personalities from the realms of politics, society, and commerce.

Her private salons were renowned, serving as forums where the world's elite convened for talks that frequently affected public discourse.

Harriman's status as a matriarch of the political and social elite endured. Her residence in Paris was a focus for world leaders, diplomats, and high-profile personalities. Despite her diminished public exposure, she was regularly consulted on topics of diplomacy and policy.

Her ability to negotiate the complicated web of international relations and her unique insight into the subtleties of political maneuvering kept her in the loop of global events.

Advocacy and Public Service

Pamela's passion for public service remained unabated. She got active with various humanitarian groups and causes, utilizing her network and influence to advocate topics near her heart. Her engagement with groups focusing on education, the arts, and women's rights emphasized her determination to make an impact outside the political world.

One prominent accomplishment was her role in the formation of the Pamela Harriman Foundation, which sponsored many charity endeavors. This foundation was a monument to her persistent conviction in leveraging her riches and influence to assist significant causes. Through the foundation, Harriman was able to express her love for charity and leave a legacy of kindness and assistance for people in need.

Legacy of Power, Passion, and Politics

Pamela Harriman's legacy is a complicated tapestry fashioned from strands of power, emotion, and politics. Her life narrative is one of amazing successes and lasting impact, showing a rare combination of charm, strategic skill, and personal attraction.

Influence and Power

Harriman's impact stretched well beyond her public presence. Her capacity to change political landscapes and influence major players in government and industry was unrivaled. As a behind-the-scenes power broker, she played a significant part in important events in 20th-century politics.

Her efforts in changing American political dynamics, notably via her participation in the Democratic Party and her support for Bill Clinton's ascendancy to the president, were essential in establishing a new age of American leadership.

Her strategic savvy was obvious in her ability to interact with and influence prominent persons across numerous domains. From her early days as Winston Churchill's daughter-in-law to her subsequent responsibilities in U.S. politics, Harriman exhibited an amazing aptitude to traverse and manipulate the corridors of power. Her legacy in this respect is a tribute to her skilled management of relationships and her strong awareness of political dynamics.

Passion and Personal Connections

Pamela Harriman's personal life was distinguished by a deep involvement with the world around her. Her ties with powerful individuals, her devotion to cultural and social issues, and her busy social life all reflect her desire to live fully and have an effect.

Her connections with important personalities, like the Kennedys, Frank Sinatra, and Truman Capote, illustrate her capacity to relate on a very intimate level with those who affected public life.

These contacts were not only social connections but key pieces of her network that allowed her to wield power and impact change. Her enthusiasm for the arts, fashion, and high society was matched by her devotion to utilizing her platform to promote issues she believed in.

Political Legacy

Pamela Harriman's political legacy is distinguished by her contributions to diplomacy, political strategy, and public service. Her time as U.S. Ambassador to France highlighted her capacity to handle intricate international connections and impact global affairs. Her efforts in fostering peace and developing U.S.-European ties were important successes that underlined her knowledge and dedication to diplomatic excellence.

Her involvement in rejuvenating the Democratic Party and helping Bill Clinton's climb to the presidency is a defining feature of her political legacy. Harriman's strategic vision and political cunning played a vital part in defining contemporary American politics. Her ability to recognize and encourage budding political leaders, combined with her influence in important political circles, left a lasting effect on the political scene.

The Enduring Impact

Pamela Harriman's death in 1997 marked the end of a magnificent life, yet her legacy continues to be felt. Her legacy is remembered not just for her high-profile accomplishments but also for the subtler, sometimes overlooked ways in which she changed the globe.

Her contributions to politics, her humanitarian activities, and her lively personal relationships all combine to create a multidimensional legacy that remains.

In thinking about her life, it becomes evident that Pamela Harriman was more than a socialite or diplomat; she was a tremendous force whose impact spanned countries and decades. Her narrative is one of power handled with delicacy, love pursued with fervor, and politics managed with tact. Her life is a monument to the influence one person can have on the world, altering history with a mix of charm, strategy, and unrelenting dedication.

Conclusion

Pamela Harriman's life was a lesson in the art of persuasion, a tribute to the power of charm, strategy, and unrelenting determination. From the dazzling salons of Paris to the corridors of American power, she constructed a tale of political skill and personal appeal that transformed the 20th century. Her tale is one of overcoming prejudice, leveraging connections, and navigating the complicated dance of foreign diplomacy and home politics.

As the daughter-in-law of Winston Churchill, she first looked doomed to stay in the shadows of history. Yet, Harriman's unrelenting determination and ability converted her from a recognized socialite into a powerful political force. Her jobs, from wartime diplomat to

Democratic strategist, were not only about beauty and intrigue but about making strategic judgments that resonated on a worldwide scale.

Harriman's legacy is varied. It is a legacy of power utilized with caution, passion directed into worthy causes, and politics maneuvered with unrivaled ability. Her capacity to influence and inspire, whether via direct action or behind-the-scenes manipulation, has left an indelible impression on both sides of the Atlantic.

In looking at her life, we see more than a narrative of sumptuous events and high-profile partnerships. We observe a woman who, through brilliance and persistence, played a vital part in molding contemporary history. Pamela Harriman's narrative reasserts that genuine power frequently rests not in the spotlight but in the quiet, strategic moments that decide the path of countries. Her legacy survives as a reminder of the remarkable effect one human can have on the world.

Printed in Great Britain
by Amazon

48495343R00079